LET THERE BE GOD

*An Approach to Deity
for Thinking Man*

Other books by the same author:

THE INNERMOST CHAMBER
Im Innersten Raum

COLLECTED POEMS

THE SILVERY FLUTE
Poems for children

(Obtainable through The Merwin Art Shop,
286 York Street, New Haven, Conn.)

LET THERE BE GOD

AN APPROACH TO DEITY FOR THINKING MAN

by

OLGA ERBSLOH MULLER

PHILOSOPHICAL LIBRARY

New York

Printed in the United States of America

To the memory of my husband,
who made this book possible.

CONTENTS

Chapter

LET THERE BE GOD

*An Approach to Deity
for Thinking Man*

INTRODUCTION

Man stands upon this earth in the white light of reality.
But the organs of perception with which he is endowed do
not permit him to receive this light in all its purity. He
can accept it only through the medium of his senses, a
prism where it is broken up into a flight of colors. No
matter how white the radiance about him, he perceives
only the rainbow hues given him through his senses. Yet
man has a yearning for the pure white light. This yearning has developed his science and philosophy. And through
the lens of science and philosophy, the rainbow colors
of the prism of the senses are recombined into the white
light of truth. The process is not perfect; much light is
lost through imperfections in the prism and the lens.
Truth never can *be* reality; but, in an ever increasing
measure, man's yearning for the white light can be ful-
filled.

"This have I dared!" said Ulrich von Hutten, having vowed never to forsake the truth. For those who dare as he did, this book is written. It does not matter that today we can no longer follow his concepts and subscribe to his creed. What matters is that in the face of duress and threats of hell-fire, he had the courage to maintain his spiritual integrity — clinging to the truth as he saw it — without fear or favor of man or God. They who reverence the truth will refuse to be seduced by any faith, no matter how beautiful or satisfying, and will resolutely shut out of their minds all that cannot be in some measure substantiated before the bar of their intellect. They will not close their eyes, no matter how alluring the promise of the dream that comes to the blind. Not without homesickness for the beautiful images of man's childhood, they will abstain from the worship of idols whose god-head their intellect can no longer accept. At the same time they will be humble in the knowledge that the light by which they are guided may be a will-o'-the-wisp whose falsehood will be plain to later generations. They know well that they are taking this chance, but they cling to the supreme desire to keep their minds clean of beliefs founded only upon longing. They admit but one last faith: If there is a God, He would want me to think.

This book is dedicated to the inquiry: what dare we admit of spiritual hope and still keep clean? There is no final answer to this question. The answer will recede before us as does the horizon before the man who marches on. Nevertheless, a temporary answer must continually be made. We must render account to ourselves at every moment of where we stand. Agnosticism is spiritual death. In

12

the humble consciousness of our final ignorance, let us try to discover how far we have come. Reality we cannot grasp, but we know our own love of the truth.

Thought is man's highest function. It is not only our right but our duty to think. And the supreme exercise of that function is thought about the nature of God. Those who consider this wicked or are simply bored by it, need read no further. This book is not for them. It is written for those who find themselves, willingly or unwillingly, outside the confines of a childhood faith and, knowing themselves in a strange country, still hold it their duty to go on seeking a goal of whose very existence they are no longer certain. They do not give up. They continue to advance by what light they may find to seek God, even though they may have been intellectually forced to deny Him. They seek Him in good works, they seek Him in art, they seek Him in science through his creation. The road they travel is often tragic and lonely. Have you ever been so happy that you wanted to fall down on your knees and pour out your soul in thankfulness to the creator of that happiness and then looked about you and found no creator but blind chance? To the brave man this is an experience far more tragic than finding himself in trouble and then having no one to whom to go whining for help. The strong soul needs God more for his exaltation than for his succor. The strong soul can perhaps face the last extremity of despair alone, but he needs God for the painful intensity of his experience of love, of beauty, of happiness. And the strong soul, even having denied God, will never give up seeking Him.

Man throughout the ages has tried various approaches

to the finding of God. There is, for example, the approach through mystical yearning; also, the approach of pure reason through philosophy. Finally, and latest to be adopted, there is the approach to the finding of God through the study of the creation.

We who think cannot permit ourselves the approach through mystical yearning. If it is more immediate, it leaves the door wide open to self-deceit and all manner of falsehood. A clean and self-controlled thinker will refuse to enter the fog of emotional excesses that this approach demands.

The approach of pure reason also offers pitfalls. Descartes began by doubting everything and ended by finding a definite physical seat for the soul! Speculation towering upon speculation, without any check against sensory experience in between, is a structure upon which modern man will refuse to place his trust. Moreover, the answers given by pure philosophy have been so many and so varied — so divergent from one another — that one would not know whom to trust for guidance. There is no philosophy, there are only a large number of philosophies. Our senses form our only direct contact with the external world, and to leave the evidence of our senses out of an estimate of this world is throwing away the only tool which we have. Intuition has its place where sensory evidence ceases, but in the face of that evidence we dare not trust it. If our senses are untrustworthy, how much more our reason, which has only grown up through the experience and tutelage of our senses. What is intuition after all but subconscious reasoning from the previously collected evidence of our senses? — unless, indeed, we beg the whole question by assuming a divine power that gives us that intuition. So-called pure reasoning is no more pure than the experience which supplies the data for our reasoning. When it is forcibly divorced from that experience — outwardly, at least, for in the last analysis it can never be finally divorced — it becomes a tottering structure whose foundations have been cut away.

There is, finally, the study of God through creation. Here at last is the firm ground where we shall not lose ourselves either in emotionalism or in the pitfalls of our own limited reason. The method of science, with its continual experimental checks, is the only one which offers any hope of arriving at ultimate truth. But even here we must be continually on the lookout for human error. We must be prepared at any moment to sacrifice cherished conclusions when the basis upon which they rest has been undermined by new discovery. We must keep our thinking clean of wishful conclusions and go ahead, step by slow step, admitting it when we come to the limits of our knowledge. Science is far from perfect, but it is the best guide that we have to clear thinking.

Unfortunately, the limits of science are reached early when we are searching for God, so early indeed that many have thought it not the proper tool to employ in the search. Nevertheless, we shall follow science as far as it leads us, even though the conclusions we draw may be only negative. We shall accept the whole body of scientific thought and go on from there, for the proper sphere for speculation lies beyond the boundaries of science. Here we are free to draw conclusions from what we (temporarily) regard as fact. Here we may make deductions and build structures of thought. Here is the sphere of pure reason. Here we may even allow voice to our emotions, for after all, emotions are founded in nature and, as the voice of our blood, are not lightly to be disregarded.

Where the possibility of fact-finding ceases, there we may, in all honesty and cleanliness of mind, go forward, led by our yearning, even through mysticism, toward God.

CHAPTER II

THERE IS NO GOD

What is God?

God is a spirit who has power over man and creation. He is both omnipotent and good. There have been lesser gods at one time or another accepted by various religions and philosophies, but an all-powerful and good God is surely the only one whom thinking man would be willing to worship. A good God who is not all-powerful might enlist the love and loyalty of man, but not his worship. A God who is not good, no matter what His power, will be repudiated by courageous man.

This then is the definition of God. Is there such a being?

We turn to science. Science, however, has no definite answer to give us. There are probably as many scientists today with a religious outlook as there are with an atheistic or an agnostic one. Science, particularly physical science, which used to be the discipline most sure of itself, has of recent years learned a new humility.

Says A. S. Eddington in his *Nature of the Physical World*:

"The symbolic nature of the entities of physics is now generally recognized, and the scheme of physics is now formulated in such a way as to make it almost self-evident that it is a partial aspect of something wider." And again (p. 275):

"The modern scientific theories have broken away from the common standpoint which identifies the real with the concrete."

Herbert D. Curtis in *Modern Physical Science: Its Relation to Religion* says:

"Somewhat to his surprise, the modern scientist finds that he has gradually and without prevision reached a point where he is permitting himself, even demanding, beliefs and theories which involve the transcendental and the infinite."

And from the biological viewpoint, Thomas White Patrick in *Idealistic Confessions of a Behaviorist*:

"The history of evolution has been a history of new forms and new functions. It bears none of the marks of a wholly mechanistic process, since it transcends mechanism at every new step."

Science, then, gives us the sanction to go on with our exploration, but beyond this it offers no further help. From here on we must deal frankly with "mind stuff", as Eddington calls it, and rely only on reason to be our guide.

Shall we go on?

There have been many philosophical proofs presented for the existence of God. They derive their validity from various premises, but they are all very much alike in one respect. They prove the existence of something which they call "God" and, later, having proved this, they expand the definition of the term "God" to cover whatever they wish to include — often something far beyond the limits of what they have originally proved. In this way they arrive at a good and omnipotent God whose existence they could not possibly have proved had they set out to do so in the first place.

There is no space here for individual examination of these theories. Let us rather look directly at the facts of nature and see what can be deduced from them.

There are some who would derive the existence of a good and omnipotent God from the glory of creation. Nature is perfect, they argue; therefore, the creator must be perfect. Let us leave aside for a moment the question of how creation can be conceived to have taken place, for reason and science are no better at explaining ultimate origins than is faith. Let us turn simply to the major premise of those who believe that they are able to establish the existence of God by reason. "Nature is perfect" — what an overwhelming act of faith is required to believe this! Anyone who succeeds in convincing himself that nature is perfect should have no difficulty in believing every miracle of the Bible. An act of faith is already committed in the acceptance of the major premise, and the 'proof' of the existence of a good and omnipotent God can be made to follow harmlessly. But we must keep our eyes open. Nature is cruel, wasteful and niggardly at the same time, inefficient, ruthless, capricious, unjust, wanton — anything but perfect. It is only the selfless, stupendous courage of man that makes him persist in regarding nature as glorious in the face of pain and death; that, and his sense of beauty. For nature to man is overwhelmingly beautiful, so beautiful that often it seems that nothing else matters. Man is ready to adore it and to suffer all things in his adoration. But is it not man who is admirable in his selfless, courageous adoration rather than the object of his worship, which cherishes him at one moment and playfully wills his destruction at the next?

The great act of faith required to believe that nature is perfect is not for thinking man, who has his eyes open. As for the statement that all pain is the result of breaking natural laws, one very simple example will suffice to show up its impossible nature: A woman giving birth to a child is obeying natural law; yet she suffers agonies. Pain is itself a part of natural law. "Eat and be eaten" is one of the most fundamental of the laws of nature.

Moreover, even if it could be maintained that the breaking of natural laws is the sole cause of pain, we would still have a problem on our hands. Man is in great part ignorant of natural laws. Would a good and omnipotent God punish man for ignorance?

Wherever we turn to establish the existence of a good and omnipotent God, we are at once faced with the problem of pain. It seems hardly necessary to go into individual examples to prove the presence of pain in the world. Pain is so universally accepted as the *sine-qua-non* of human life that the mere mention of it as a problem may cause surprise. There is no birth without pain, no life and no death. Pain, physical and spiritual, is a very condition of living. If the human race in spite of this universal agony continues to consider life as good, it is only because of its great courage.

Who has not seen an innocent baby suffer? Who has not seen life cut off in its prime and decrepit, agonized old age survive instead? Who has not seen justified hope laid in ruins, love mocked, conscientious effort thwarted? Who has not seen inexplicable suffering in the faces of those he loves? Who has not seen meaningless agony in the dumb creatures of nature?

And yet man, instead of repudiating the entire system which makes such pain possible, only searches humbly for some kind of explanation. Various explanations have been offered.

Pain is the punishment for man's sins.

Even Christian doctrine with its emphasis on sin is not so blind as to claim that individual visitations of pain are the punishment for individual sins. Rather, each individual in his liability to pain is made responsible for the sins of all. Unquestioning, Christ accepted the burden of all sin, and his followers, with 'Pater, peccavi', believe they have solved the problem of pain. Every true believer is in his own flesh the sacrificial lamb of God so that he may hold his God blameless. Being thus made perfect by the sacrifice of his worshipers, God in turn offers forgiveness and, after death, fellowship in His own blamelessness to man, who has accepted the blame. Would a good and omnipotent God make His creatures suffer for something He might have prevented?

Would we deliberately put temptation in the way of our children and then punish them if they fall? Presumably, God is all-knowing. He knows that man, tempted, will fall and make himself liable to punishment. Would we put our children under conditions where they would be bound to commit grievous sin, so that we might go through the rigmarole of redemption, forgiveness and final reward, all brought to pass in agony, that they might love us the more? A god who permits this is not a good God.

Pain does not exist; we only imagine it. It is our error.

This is probably the only logical deduction to be drawn from the premise of the existence of a good and omnipotent God. The minute we question the premise, of course, the whole structure falls. Moreover, if we are arguing from the conclusions of Christian Science back to the existence of a good and omnipotent God, as we are doing here, we find that the same thing applies to Christian Science as applies to Christianity in general. Whether you call the trouble sin or error makes very little difference. The fact remains that millions of human beings suffer. Christian Science would make it a little bit easier to get out of that suffering, but why would a good and omnipotent God institute it in the first place? And here we come directly to another explanation of pain.

Pain is a preparation for a future state of perfection.

Of all the theories invented by man so that he may hold his God blameless, this is the most pathetically courageous. Man actually sinks his teeth into his bitter suffering and insists on deriving from it an impetus toward nobility of soul. And here, for once, man has carried over into his own ethics what he condones in his God. We are often hard on our children in the hope of improving them. This argument, therefore, is the hardest to answer.

However, one obvious answer comes to mind: If pain is to fit human beings for future perfection, it should be their special prerogative. But we find dumb animals, who are not to be included in moral perfection, suffering together with man. What can be the explanation of that? This objection may, however, be considered too petty to answer so magnificent an idea. It is true that there are human beings who wring nobility of character from extreme pain. It is true that there are those who succeed in sublimating their suffering until it becomes almost happiness. Many martyrs live and die with a smile upon their lips. Is this, then, the true and justifiable explanation of pain?

Is it not rather proof of the courage and the strength of soul of man that he is able to convert even his suffering to good? Would a good and omnipotent God have to invent this cruel means of leading His children to the light? If we are hard on our children, it is only because all life is hard and we seek to prepare them for it. We permit them to suffer only because there is no life without suffering. If we could manage to teach them in any other

23

way we would certainly do so. We are not omnipotent, and the omnipotent God who looks on at the suffering of His people, because that is the way He has chosen to teach them, is not good.

Pain is the result of the devil's work.

Another explanation that has been offered for the presence of pain in the world is that which traces it to the existence of a powerful evil principle — the devil or some such figure. This needs hardly a word to dispose of it. Obviously a God who permits the existence of a devil to tempt and harass man is either not omnipotent or not good. The notion that a good and omnipotent God would allow a principle of evil to exist and make sport of man is so utterly immoral that it hardly needs a word of refutation.

There are those who would be willing to worship a God who considers man beneath His notice, who is so taken up with transcendental affairs that the sufferings of the poor creatures crawling about on earth do not reach His attention. But God omnipotent must be omniscient. If He cannot be bothered with what He Himself has created, again He is not good. What is to be admired in this theory is, once more, the overwhelming courage and aspiration of man who would attach his loyalty to a cruel being who in turn would have none of him.

Finally, the believers in a good and omnipotent God must take refuge in the safe assertion that God's ways are inscrutable. This, of course, is an utterly unanswerable argument; but for the man who has resolved to think for himself, it has no validity. There are those who prefer to

24

believe at whatever cost. Let them be happy. A God whose cruelties are incomprehensible is surely even less good than one who might offer some explanation. Thinking man must therefore refuse to close his eyes before the Being he seeks to worship.

There is no good and omnipotent God.

This is the tragedy of man
that he can find no peace or joy
save in the seeking after God
and that there is no God.
Only desire is divine.

THE CURVE

Upon a system of coordinates
We plot the course of our advancing lives.
One line across the page a little space
Is run to tell our briefly numbered years;
The other rises upward from the base
And passes on into the far unknown,
Dimension this of what man calls his soul.

We start at zero and the curve runs on
Relentlessly across the charted page.
We cannot bid it halt nor can extend,
(So short and fixed) the horizontal line.
Only in height and depth may we be free,
Explore but never fathom all the deep,
Can stretch our hands up to the far beyond
And in one horizontal moment brief
Can reach into the limitless sublime.

Why should we mourn because the curve is short,
Because each moment passes swiftly by,
When all the glorious height and depth is ours,
When we that die may know the infinite,
Godlike, eternal in another sense?

CHAPTER III

CREATION

Does man stand alone in an empty cosmos ruled by blind chance? How did this cosmos come to be? Again, science offers no final help.

It leads us back through the stages of evolution, back beyond the beginnings of consciousness, back beyond the origins of life — in no even and clear path, but with great gaps of explanation in between — to a playground of atoms, and there it leaves us with no ultimate explanation of beginnings.

Let us then admit at once that about first origins we can say nothing. We have come here to the absolute limits of human understanding. A first cause uncaused is entirely beyond our conception, as is happening without causality. We can go down the eons of development of the stars, down beyond the first origins of the earth, but in the end

27

we shall always come upon the inexplicable. "In the beginning was the word" or chaos or God. All these statements are equally meaningless in any real sense.

Why not assume, then, the presence of a creating God? We have shown in the last chapter that such a God, while He might be omnipotent, would not be good and that therefore man would not be willing to worship Him. For the purpose of our inquiry, therefore, it will do us no good to make such an assumption. Moreover, there are definite reasonable objections.

In a cosmos where strict causality has been abandoned by science, perhaps it is foolish to ask for a first cause. We do not even know quite what we mean when we ask for this. We cannot, even in our imagination, grasp a cause outside the cosmos. The cosmos comprises everything that is knowable, imaginable. We cannot apprehend any agency outside the cosmos that would have a bearing upon it. This would require an act of blind faith which we have renounced. It is equally incomprehensible, perhaps, but far more reasonable to assume that creation is from within. Since nothing can be proved to the contrary, we have a perfect right to make this assumption.

And creation is by no means completed. It has been regarded as completed because, according to science, the sum total of matter-energy appears to have been constant from the beginning; but this is, after all, only the building-stone of creation. If the world were now composed merely of unorganized matter-energy, we would have to assume that its creation was completed in its earliest origins. But there are entirely new factors that have entered. There is life, there is consciousness, there is spirit. These are the great gaps in the orderly explanation which science offers of the origins of the present-day world; and these are the evidences of a continuing creative force at work in the cosmos. Even should man at some time learn the secret of creating life from inanimate matter, it would prove merely that he has come to a deeper understanding of the process of creation, rather than that such a process does not exist.

It is in the realm of organization, then, that we may say creation is still proceeding. This can be called evolution, but we must bear in mind the great leaps it has made: life from inertness, consciousness from the unconscious. May not these be called acts of creation? Call it evolution or creation — at any rate it is a process still proceeding, a process that shows no signs of stopping. There is nothing more mysterious in assuming a continuing creation than in postulating a completed one. On the contrary, it seems far more reasonable to suppose that the forces which formed the cosmos are still at work than to imagine that they should have committed an act in the dim past and then have faded completely out of the picture. We have a perfect right to assume that creation is continuous and still at work today. Moreover, with the abandonment of strict causality by science, the last objection to such a view vanishes.

Creation is proceeding in a direction. This is proved by what Eddington calls "time's arrow" — entropy.* En-

*As Lecomte du Noüy has shown in his book, *Human Destiny,* the increasing organization of living beings is inexplicable under the law of entropy. This is one more of the unexplained mysteries.

tropy, which is a measure of the random element throughout the cosmos, is continually growing. There is no returning from that. It proves beyond the shadow of a doubt
that creation has a direction.

Creation, then, is from within, is continuous, and is
going in a direction. The driving force which spurs creation we shall call the cosmic will. This is no metaphysical
conception. It is merely a convenient name for the power
that rules the stars in their courses, the onward push behind evolution, the life force. It is the basis of chemical
affinities, the force that awakened consciousness in sleeping matter, the sanction of all natural laws. Everything
that *is,* is because of the cosmic will.

Have we then come merely to another name for God?
No. At the outset we repudiated any God who was not
at once good and omnipotent. The cosmic will is neither
good nor entirely omnipotent.

That it is not good, is evident from the evil that results
from its impetus. The same condition that we found in
our search for a good God applies here.

That the cosmic will is not entirely omnipotent is far
more difficult to prove.

The cosmic will has done what it pleased. It has created
matter-energy, has bound it under self-imposed natural
laws, has created life, has evolved consciousness. Is this
not omnipotence? But it has also created a world of conflict, a cosmos of continual struggle of opposing forces, a
world of mutual destruction, in spite of its natural laws,
without harmony, without apparent purpose. It has cre-

ated man, a being capable of the sublime, and left him subject to sin, decay and death. The cosmic will has played. It is an inward instability in the cosmic will rather than any outward limitation which leads us to deny its complete omnipotence. It is, one might almost say, a moral consideration rather than a question of physical power. Omnipotence implies omniscience, and what shall we think of an omniscience that creates a world in continual conflict with itself, continually thwarting its own ends, destroying with one hand what it builds up with the other, as does the actual world. It is the disharmony in the natural world which leads us again to deny to the cosmic will complete omnipotence. True, the religions have accepted the omnipotence of God on these same terms, but there has always entered the proposition, "the ways of God are inscrutable." We have resolved to reject this statement and to examine nature without prejudice. The cosmic will is not omnipotent — at least, *not yet*.

The cosmic will, then, is physical necessity; it is nature, it is fate. But it is not God.

Thus, we find man conscious, aspiring in the midst of a cosmos still developing from within under the impetus of a playing force.

What, then, is man's role in creation?

31

Chapter IV

MAN IN THE COSMOS

Man stands at the highest point in the scale of evolution. However perfect the lower creatures are, however well adapted to their particular conditions of environment (and some of them, notably the insects, may be better adapted to their particular conditions than man is to his), there can be no doubt that man is the highest creature yet evolved. If we adopt the human scale of values in making this statement, who is there to gainsay us? A perfect plant may be perfect in its own way, but man has dominion over all the creatures of nature. Not only that, man has one outstanding quality which puts him above all other creatures. That is his development of consciousness to a point unknown below man — and with consciousness, spirit.

What is spirit and how shall we define it? It is a word

33

far better understood in the adjective than in the noun. While we use 'spiritual' freely and know perfectly what we mean by it, the term 'spirit' is far more difficult to handle. In its origin it might be defined as any activity of man that goes beyond the demands and needs of his physical life. In this sense, all play is spiritual activity. Even the miser's love for his gold might be called such. It is, then, an activity, or rather, perhaps, the energy under-lying that activity — energy that leads to activity transcending the physical needs of man. Transcending! Here is the word we want. Spirit goes beyond! Arising from the material, from the food we eat, it surpasses the material to create a realm of its own. Is there such a thing?

Eddington says in his *The Nature of the Physical World*: "The sanction for correlating a 'real' physical world to certain feelings of which we are conscious, does not seem to differ in any essential respect from the sanction for correlating a spiritual domain to another side of our personality."

That is to say: There is no absolute proof of the exist-ence outside our consciousness of a physical world. Many philosophers have denied such existence. If we insist on be-lieving in an independent physical world, there is merely physical experience to 'prove' it. In the same way exactly there is spiritual experience to prove the existence of spirit. We may know it by its manifestations.

Spirit manifests itself in religion, in art, in pure science, in real love, in serenity in the face of trouble, in love of nature, in strength of character. It means nothing that these things can be partially explained away by various

34

physical means. Taken together, they have a common quality, a *leitmotif,* which defies physical explanation and can only be abstracted under the term 'spirit'.

Spirit is one of those words which are not understood except by immediate experience. It cannot be defined any more than light can be explained to the blind. To define light as vibrations in the ether, or what not, gives no explanation of the experience of sight. Nor can we explain the experience of spirit to the spiritually blind. The man born blind is at liberty to consider sight as a peculiar delusion of the seeing. He realizes that it gives them strange powers, that with the help of sight they are able to accomplish miraculous things, but, having no experience of the phenomenon, he is able to consider it a kind of hysteria (a world which is a label and in this case means nothing). He is at liberty to deny the existence of light altogether.

What, then, is spirit? We know its origin, we can discover and list its manifestations, but the word itself escapes definition. Let him who is not blind, understand.

Shall we deny spirit to the other organisms altogether? Does not a dog's love and loyalty to his master go far beyond his physical necessities? Shall we deny spirit to a perfect tree, to a rose? It is not a simple question, for it can never be ascertained how much of the virtue or the beauty of a thing lies in the eyes of the beholder. Is it we who endow a collection of cells with a transcendental meaning, or is there mysteriously in this aggregation of protoplasm a yearning toward perfection? There is no insult to man, no degradation to spirit in placing its origins below the human level. It must certainly be considered a product of consciousness, but who shall say at what level rudimentary consciousness arises? And at precisely what level of consciousness spirit began to evolve is another question that will find no answer. Perhaps spirit is co-existent with consciousness. Thus, rudimentary consciousness would mean a rudimentary form of spirit. In death, at least, the two merge into one. The loss of consciousness in death means the loss of spirit, at least to the individual body.

Not, then, categorically denying some form of spirit to the lower beings in the scale of evolution, at the same time it cannot be controverted that in man spirit comes to a purer, more intense expression than in any other creature. Man is the highest form of life.

We must go further in an analysis of consciousness. Consciousness is the deepest mystery of creation. Millikan in his *Evolution in Science and Religion,* says: "The most amazing thing in all life, the greatest miracle there is, is the fact that a mind has got here at all, 'created out of the dust of the earth' ". We shall never be able to understand how it was awakened in sleeping matter. To some it is the very proof of all existence (Descartes), to some it is the proof of the existence of God. Indeed, it is difficult not to ascribe to a fact so uterly incomprehensible something of a metaphysical nature.

We know that there is a connection between our physical structure, our brain, and consciousness. We even know that electricity bears some relation to the phenomenon, but precisely what that connection and relation is we have no means of knowing, probably no means of ever learning. We must accept it as the greatest stroke of genius of the playing cosmic will. If we do not ascribe it immediately to metaphysical causes, it is probably only because we know its physical seat, because we can cancel it out at will (through anaesthesia), because 'we have watched the changes that are wrought in it through changes in the brain. But that does not make it any more comprehensible.

Whether we regard consciousness as a gadget uselessly superimposed upon an otherwise orderly material universe or whether we regard it as the veiled basis of all reality — even the material — the contemplation of consciousness at once opens the door to metaphysical possibilities. We shall try here to keep as far as possible from metaphysical entanglements and humbly accept consciousness as the physicist does his electrons, asking not "what is it?", but "how does it operate?"

What is the relation between consciousness and the cosmic will?

According to our definition of the cosmic will, it has created consciousness. That is, the cosmic will, continuing to create through evolution, has *become conscious*. But the highest seat of that consciousness is man. Man, therefore, is not only the creature of the cosmic will, he is also its *bearer*. The cosmic will, conscious in man, continues its creation. *Man through consciousness becomes a partaker in creation.* This is the central theme of our analysis.

Man, partaker in creation, has evolved spirit or, at least, has brought it to its highest flowering up to this point. We have placed the origins of spirit firmly in the material world, but its implications reach far into the metaphysical. We may shy from concepts that have this mysterious nature. It would be blind, however, to deny the reality beneath. If spirit is incomprehensible, so is consciousness which gives rise to it. The attempt to base an explanation of life upon conditioned reflexes is fully as absurd as the concept of a heaven populated by white-robed and musical angels. It explains a great deal, but it simply fails to explain reality as we know it. Matter, having given rise to life, having awakened to consciousness, has produced that overtone which we need have no shame in calling spirit. Any description of the phenomenon in other terms is simply an effort to avoid the issue. Spirit, metaphysical as it may be, has a reality at least as actual as that of matter, a reality inherent in life and thus inherent in matter itself. With the evolution of consciousness, that flame which is spirit has been kindled in matter. If we cannot bridge the gap between matter and spirit, it is only one of the fundamental mysteries. To deny spirit because we do not understand its origin is willfully to shut our eyes to one of the greatest aspects of reality.

Striving to be as clear as we can, we can today conceive of spirit only as a certain mysterious energy arising from matter. And to accept its material origin is in no way to impair its awe-ful significance. Let it rather awaken in us a reverence for all reality.

Man is bound to the earth and yet at the same time possessed of spirit. He can no longer claim the innocence and immortality of matter. His head is in the clouds, he can be no longer sure of the solid ground beneath him. At the same time he has not found his wings, cannot exist in the pure medium of spirit to which he constantly aspires. It is only in passing moments that he seems to achieve the freedom of spiritual life. There are moments in man's life when he seems to lay hold of a transcendant reality — indeed, eternity itself, not in the sense of permanence but in the sense of timelessness. Every man oriented toward spirit has known such moments of supreme experience to which time can add nothing, from which fate can take nothing away. It is this experience which gives us the courage to say that if we can lay hold upon it, eternity is here and now. It is true that this conception requires a deep mysticism.

Let us conceive of man's life as drawn up on a system of coordinates. Starting at zero, the horizontal axis runs briefly across the blank page and comes to an end. This is the measure of man's days of life. But the vertical axis, the measure upon which he shall plot the curve of his spirit, runs upward and downward to the immeasurable beyond. In one brief horizontal moment he may reach down to fathomless depths, may attain to heights that are boundless, may lay hold upon eternity. It is in the midst of life that we may look forward to being taken up into heaven.

Why, then, should we mourn because the time-axis of our lives is fixed and short? Eternity is not to be measured in time. The measure of eternity is a reality of the spirit.

Earth and spirit are inextricably bound together, but their realities, arising from the common zero, diverge in different senses. And in the sense of spirit man can lay hold upon eternity.

39

Man, co-creator with the cosmic will, can create spirit even to eternity.

CHAPTER V

ETHICS

In a world empty of God, what sanctions remain for ethics?

If the man in the street requires a system of rewards and punishments to make him 'be good', such is not the case for the man of thought and serious striving whom we have had in mind throughout this book. Indeed, deprived of a personal God who will guide his conduct, he will seek all the more insistently for some norm by which he may be lead. Let us see what we can find.

Though many moralists have entirely neglected it, we come in any discussion of ethics first upon the problem of free will. Science has gone a long way from the complete denial of free will which seemed to be inescapable not so long ago. Eddington says:

"Strict causality is abandoned in the material world. Our ideas of the controlling laws are in process of reconstruction and it is not possible to predict what kind of form they will ultimately take; but all indications are that strict causality has dropped out permanently. This relieves the former necessity of supposing that mind is subject to deterministic law or alternately that it can suspend deterministic law in the material world."*

We have, at last, then, the sanction of science to build a structure that shall lead us to free will. Let us see how this may be achieved.

If we regard creation as completed and from without, there seems no room anywhere for free will. Spinoza's clock, once started, will run on indefinitely without the interference of man. There is no room in such a cosmos for anything save strict causality. However, we have chosen to regard creation as continuous and from within, guided by a principle which we called the cosmic will.

The cosmic will, creator of man, has awakened him to consciousness. Whereas creation before consciousness was a groping in the dark — the sleep in the womb of a babe self-mothered and self-begotten — with consciousness, a new phase of life begins. Man possessed of consciousness is no longer the mere creature of the cosmic will; he is at the same time the possessor, the exponent of the awakened will, the *co-creator!* Man not only *is* by virtue of the cosmic will, he *has* the cosmic will. And this will, free from all origins, is in man free also! Man's will is free.

* *The Nature of the Physical World.*

42

When we consider the origins of man's will, the conflicts that he is subject to at once become clear. We have claimed for the cosmic will no qualities that would guarantee peace and harmony in the world which it is creating. The cosmic will is free — even to play! It is free to create of itself a variety of manifestations, each possessed of vitality and entering into conflict one with the other, and free to bind all these divergent powers once more under its self-imposed natural laws. The play of the cosmic will — this is the principle of the universe. And man, in his dual role of creature and creator, is the battleground for the struggle of many diverse manifestations of the cosmic will.

For to say that man's will is free is by no means to claim that it is always victorious. The earlier creature wills often prove the stronger. Man, the thinking being, may thus frequently be conquered by man, the creature; but he is never *conditioned* thereby.

The higher impulses of man, then, are those of his free will, while in his lower nature he is only a creature conditioned by physical and external demands. It is in the conflict of the higher free will with the baser wills that conscience arises. It is innate, the necessary concomitant of man's dual condition. Conscience is an immediate accompaniment of even very rudimentary free will and is found early in children in its purest form. It is something entirely other than the fear of discovery and punishment. Many a child, secure from discovery, will voluntarily confess a sin and take the punishment merely at the behest of its conscience. Like other human functions, conscience may become perverted through false teachings and especially through social fears. Fundamentally, however, an attack of conscience indicates that the free higher will has been temporarily conquered by the lower wills of the mere creature.

Since conscience is innate, must it then issue the same dictates for all men? Obviously not. It would be folly and contrary to experience to suppose that all men stand at a given moment upon the same level of development and that their free wills must therefore issue similar codes. The continuous creative forces of the cosmic will will have brought some men to a higher stage than others, and their individual wills will make very different demands upon them. This at once explains the disparity in moral law and social usages of different peoples. The conscious free will of the Hottentot is not the same as that of the European. Similar and perhaps as great diversities exist between the moral impulses of individual members of the same community. Governments roughly find the least common denominator of such variant senses of right and wrong and set up the result as laws. But under these laws, each individual continues with a passionate personal conviction of what is good and what is evil. Thus, some are made heroes and some criminals. So long as they obey their own free highest will, so long as they operate as exponents of the cosmic will rather than as creautres, their consciences will hold them blameless.

Thus, it would seem that we have come farther than ever from a universally applicable ethical law. But a simple tale from the Old Testament serves to make the whole matter clear.

"And Jacob sod pottage and Esau came from the field, and he was faint:
And Esau said to Jacob, Feed me I pray thee with that same red pottage; for I am faint. . . .
And Jacob said, Sell me this day thy birthright.
And Esau said, Behold, I am at the point to die: and what profit shall this birthright do to me?
And Jacob said, Swear to me this day: and he swear unto him: and he sold his birthright unto Jacob.
Then Jacob gave Esau bread and pottage of lentils; and he did eat and drink, and rose up, and went his way; thus Esau despised his birthright."

(Genesis **XXV**, 29-34)

Evil flowers in a variety of manifestations but at the root there is only one sin: the sin of Esau.

Sin is the satisfaction with anything less than one's own supreme expression. Sin is the failure to develop to one's highest potential. Sin is the denial of spirit. Sin is death in a very real sense, death of the free self.

There are no definable sins, there is only *sin*: the failure to obey one's own highest will, the act of the creature rather than of free, conscious man.

It follows at once that the judgment of a deed is meaningless except in relation to the doer. Not the intention, not the consequence, not any extraneous code is the criterion of a deed but only the status of the individual. What in the ordinary man might be brazen selfishness may in the artist very well be his highest, hardest achievement. The heroic death in battle of the patriot is for the conscientious

45

objector sheer cowardice. No judgment is possible without a complete understanding of the individual who has committed the deed. The truth of this has long been recognized in the old, seemingly paradoxical statement: "it is not what you do that counts, but what you are."

The good life is to be sought in the sublimation of the self towards spirit. Let us examine what this means. Of course, it is in no way synonymous with selfishness. The higher interests of the self are not served by the gratification of wishes at the expense of others. They are directed toward spiritual values which often require the complete sacrifice of immediate, personal advantage. The sublimation of the self towards spirit, in each case put to purely personal interpretation, will mean very different things. For one man it will be consecration to art, for another it will be the better education of his family, for a third it will mean devotion to the state or to some individual. But in each of these varying objectives will be bound up the highest spiritual potential of which the individual's life is capable. A full understanding of this truth will supply a most powerful motive for labor and sacrifice and a complete and joyous satisfaction in devotion. No room remains for complaint or a false air of martyrdom. All striving, all suffering is labor toward the sublimation of the self. The cause, thoughtfully chosen, is the highest expression of the personal life. Christ's saying, "Whosoever shall lose his life, shall preserve it", takes on its full meaning.

Having found a philosophic basis for the conduct of life, shall we now know how to regulate the actions of the moment? It will not always be easy. There are, however, a few criteria which may be applied to a course of action to determine whether it will fall in line with the principles advanced.

The first of these is the very simple one of time. How will such and such an action appear to me in a week, in a year, in ten years? The sobering influence of this consideration may well prevent many mistakes.

The second consideration is bound up with hero-worship. Fortunate indeed is the man who finds some other to admire. Even if his admiration is based upon an illusion, it will offer a powerful moral support. We cannot admire anything foreign to our understanding, hence in what we admire will be found the key to our own possibilities of development. And if we guide our lives by projecting them upon the lives of those for whom we feel hero-worship, we may often advance beyond our previous stage of development.

The third and most important consideration is that of spiritual value. If we examine our conduct to discover what of spiritual value it is likely to create or destroy (both for ourselves and for others), we may form a very good idea as to whether it will contribute to the sublimation of our lives.

The attitude here outlined is an arduous one. It calls for constant watchfulness; it implies a continuing necessity for making delicate decision and brings with it no little danger of false steps. Far easier it is to follow a conventional moral code. But modern man is irrevocably committed to thought. In this, at least, he remembers his birthright. Let him strive to further understanding, fol-

47

lowing his free creator will, seeking not satisfaction but renewal of desire toward the highest potential of the self — spirit.

CHAPTER VI

THE FUTURE OF MAN

There are few men of profound emotional capacity who have not at some time in their lives experienced communion with God.

There are few men of honest intelligence who have not at some time come to the inescapable necessity of denying the existence of God.

These are the two extremes of experience, one as overwhelming and necessary as the other, from which there appears to be no escape. It is only by an arbitrary and not entirely honest act of the will that either experience can be forced into the background so as to leave room for the other, for few men have found it possible ultimately to reconcile the two. And yet they are both tremendous facts, not to be denied without doing violence to a part of the

49

personality. Their antithesis has constituted a major tragedy for many.

In this world so full of evil and sorrow, can there be a good and at the same time omnipotent God? Obviously the only honest answer is *no*. All philosophies that attempt to get around this fact rest, at some point or other, upon a lie. The honest man cannot escape from the fact that a good and omnipotent God could not suffer the world for one moment to remain as it is. Any excuse that is offered for such a deity places Him upon a moral plane considerably below that of His creatures, for no feeling human being would permit the suffering and injustice which life entails, no matter how magnificent his ultimate purpose. There is no escape from the conclusion: If God is conceived as omnipotent and good, *there is no God*.

And at the same time: "The Lord is my shepherd, I shall not want. . . . He restoreth my soul. . . . He leadeth me in the paths of righteousness for His name's sake. . . . I shall dwell in the house of the Lord for ever." How shall we deny the unimpeachable testimony of the millions who in their own lives *have known God?* How shall we put out of mind the awe-inspiring strength of soul of the martyrs to faith, the power to resist temptation, to bear sorrow and death with fortitude, even in men who alone are weak, the potency to conquer in the name of God? These are all facts of human experience and to refuse to accept them is, again, an act of dishonesty or at least of blindness. Nor is the potency of God confined to subjective experience alone. If we deny all the Biblical miracles as insufficiently substantiated, we yet have a mass of modern miracles which we cannot with open mind refuse to accept. Faith-healing is a fact attested to by many of the most sceptical, by all who have taken the trouble to examine the matter at first hand. To consign all this to the realm of hysteria is merely to attach an invidious label to the fact, but by no means to explain it. A hysteric is a person who, through some illness, is able to perform wonders with his body which are not possible to the ordinary man. Even so, we may say that a man inspired by faith is one who is able to perform wonders not possible to the uninspired. There is no explanation in either way of stating the fact. But the testimony of those who have communed with God is overwhelming. "God lives for I have known Him."

These, then, are the two extremes of idea between which man endeavors to find a philosophy of life. To deny either is to be dishonest or blind. How shall we accept both?

It is the thesis of this book that creation is a continuous and by no means completed process driven by mysterious potencies from within. This seems to accord with the so far discovered facts of scientific thought; more we cannot demand. We must try and find our way by such light as we have.

Returning, then, to the question before us, we have on the one hand the impossibility of the existence of a good and omnipotent God, on the other hand the amazing efficacy of the God-concept. It is faith that works miracles, faith. But what can we say with certainty about the foundation on which this faith rests? It is the God-concept with which wonders are wrought. This and this alone is the established fact. How, then, is it possible for a mere idea so to influence our lives? What is man that he can find salvation in thought alone? Man is a child of nature, a creature of the earth, bound to the earth. But nature itself has evolved life and through life, consciousness, and through consciousness, spirit. Matter has, through man, become imbued with spirit. We do not understand the mechanism of these amazing developments, but to deny them for this reason is folly. Spirit is a matter of immediate experience. We know the manifestations of spirit as we know the food that we take into our bodies, even though we may not be able to explain them. Man is possessed of spirit and it is through spirit that he knows God.

What, then, can be the meaning of the two opposed statements: (a) there is no good and omnipotent God, and (b) man knows God through his spirit? Man knows the God-concept! It is the concept of God in the human mind which achieves all that we ascribe to divine power. Wherever we use the word 'God', we may substitute 'the thought of God' without in any way invalidating the statement. The thought of God is the divine power whose existence we cannot deny. It is the concept of God of which we have immediate experience, to whose power for salvation we can testify. God lives in our own minds. It is only one step further to the conclusion: God lives as He is created in the mind of man. Communion with God is the actual creation of divine power. The act of faith *creates God!*

How can feeble man, so subject to sin, create a being that is omnipotent, that is good? The last question is the easier to answer. Man in his highest yearning *is* good. The creation of his purest sublimated spirit will be good. But omnipotent?

We must come back once more to the cosmic will. We found that it was not omnipotent because it was in continual conflict with itself and continually thwarting its own ends. Nevertheless, through all this conflict and self-thwarting there may be detected a general direction of progress, the sense of the cosmos. Physics has discovered a definite direction in creation through entropy. There are other proofs. There is the late development of life from non-life, the development of consciousness in life, and finally the development of spirit. The creating cosmic will is not likely to stop there. It will go on to further creation. Evolution will go on. *The sense of the cosmos is toward the creation of God.* And in the consciousness of man the cosmic will has created the instrument that will render this possible. Through the spirit of conscious man, the conflicts in the cosmic will will be resolved and thus will becomes free to create a good and omnipotent God. Individual man, without the power of the cosmic will behind him, would be a feeble creature indeed; but when he is acting in the sense of the cosmos and at the same time through his consciousness, resolving the conflicts and self-thwartings of the cosmic will, he becomes the creator of a good and omnipotent God.

This is the great hope of the future. Today we are still in the very earliest origins of spirit. *God is not yet.* But there are moments in the life of spiritual man when he seems to apprehend his presence. Man can create God,

For man, the experience of God is so immediate, so overwhelming, that its majesty is in no way impaired by recognizing the fact that God springs from within his own being. He is called upon only to include in his reverence for the divine a profound reverence for the human spirit and for all nature, whence human spirit springs.

Nature has evolved the human spirit and it is the human spirit which creates God. Hence, the divine springs from nature itself. It is, then, not God who has created the cosmos but the cosmos which is still in the act of creating God. For creation is not completed. Spirit is only now coming over the horizon and the day of its full glory is far hence. *Omnipotent God is not yet.* It is for man in his holy yearning to achieve Him ever more and more completely.

But, in another sense, since nothing that has not potential existence can ever have actual existence, the potential of God has been since the beginning of time. Slowly, slowly, through infinite ages, the human spirit was evolved at last to give this divine principle expression in actuality. But the potential of God has been through all the ages past. The potential of nature has created man and through him creates God. Therefore, nature, able through man to create God, must be divine; it is God potential. And creation goes on toward the fulfillment of God.

CHAPTER VII

CONCLUSION

This, then, becomes the moral obligation of every man
— to strive toward the creation of God. Those who are
still bound up in a childhood faith will do so through that
faith. From their own stage of development they labor,
though blindly, towards the creation of God. Jesus Christ,
with his great faith and his obedience to it, achieved more
than any other man before or since toward the creation of
God. Indeed, he formed the whole concept of the Christian
God as He is worshiped today. This is a great advance in
ethics over the old, stern and jealous Jehovah of the Jews.

Those who look upon the universe with seeing eyes
have the greater obligation. They must be constantly attuned to spirit and through spirit seek God.

For those who are attuned to spirit, it seems to arise

from matter continuously while life lasts. The food that we take into our bodies helps to maintain it. Our material surroundings further or impede it. It is conditioned upon matter. There is, then, this thought: If energy-matter is everlasting, as according to science, and spirit is matter in some mysterious fashion converted, must not spirit also be everlasting? As the heat generated by the heavenly bodies is lost in the abysmal cold of the stellar spaces, but never actually destroyed, must not the energies of spirit which are continually given out and those which are lost at death in the chill of the material universe be actually still in some fashion existent? Must not every spiritual effort that we give rise to in our lives go on forever, time without end? The equality of temperature of the cosmos approaches a maximum. Is it possible that the same can be said of spirit — that the entire universe is becoming suffused with spirit, that eventually in the immeasurably distant future a state of balance will be reached? And will this be the millennium?

Or is there even a possibility for the survival of individual spirit? We do not know.

God is not yet. What help, then, can we find outside our own feeble personalities to achieve Him? There is room for a certain kind of prayer even for those who do not believe in the present existence of God. It will be an inarticulate prayer, a kind of wordless openness to the striving, rising forces of the cosmos, a conscious dedication to those forces. From down in the uttermost deeps where the cosmic will first began to play with inanimate atoms comes the strength which will lead through consciousness, through spirit, toward God.

It is through spiritualizing our lives that we achieve God — through sublimating our passions into real love, sublimating our daily work into a higher spiritual striving, sublimating our affections and emotions into harmony with the love of God. There will be no room in the God-oriented heart for petty passions. They will wither before the sun of the contemplation of God. It is in the whole orientation of our lives, rather than in any single act, that we may hope to achieve God. It is not enough to do good and eschew evil. That is only righteousness. The creation of God demands a constant attitude of the spirit. In this attitude we will find strength of soul and a joyous power for devotion to any cause oriented toward God. We will have the strength to deeds which, without this orientation, would be impossible. We will have behind us all the rising, striving forces of the cosmos which labors toward the creation of God. We dare not fail.

There is no God. But man, conscious creator with the cosmic will, shall say: "Let there be God!" And spirit, rising out of its material origins through consciousness, shall strengthen and purify itself, shall infuse the whole universe, shall become God!

God shall be!